Se Ri
Pak

Driven to Win

BY
MARK STEWART

THE MILLBROOK PRESS
BROOKFIELD, CONNECTICUT

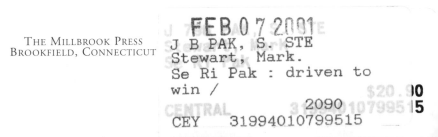

M

THE MILLBROOK PRESS

Produced by
BITTERSWEET PUBLISHING
John Sammis, President
and
TEAM STEWART, INC.

Series Design and Electronic Page Makeup by
JAFFE ENTERPRISES
Ron Jaffe

Researched and Edited by Mariah Morgan
Special thanks to Mike May, Steve Foehl, and Mike Smigie

All photos courtesy
AP/ Wide World Photos, Inc.
except the following:
AllSport, Andy Lyons Squire — Cover
The following image is from the collection of Team Stewart:
The New York Times Company Magazine Group, Inc.(1998) — Page 40

Printed in the United States of America

Published by

The Millbrook Press, Inc.
2 Old New Milford Road
Brookfield, Connecticut   06804

Visit us at our Web site — http://www.millbrookpress.com

Library of Congress Cataloging-in-Publication Data

Stewart, Mark.
    Se Ri Pak: driven to win / by Mark Stewart
    p.   cm.   — (Golf's new wave)
    Includes index.
    Summary: A biography of the young Korean woman who is breaking records on America's
professional golf tour..
    ISBN 0-7613-1519-5 (lib. bdg.)   — ISBN 0-7613-1334-6 (pbk.)
    1. Pak, Se Ri — Juvenile literature. 2. Golfers — Korea (South) Biography — Juvenile literature.
3. Women golfers — Korea (South) Biography — Juvenile literature. [1. Pak, Se Ri. 2. Golfers.
3. Women Biography.] I. Title. II. Series.
GV964.P25S84 2000
796.352'092--dc21
[B]   99-31695
                                                                   CIP

pbk: 1 3 5 7 9 10 8 6 4 2
lib: 1 3 5 7 9 10 8 6 4 2

Contents

Rough Dad, Tough Kid

"I had to teach her how tough life is. You must be steel-hearted to survive."

— JOON CHUL PAK

In the Republic of South Korea, a father's will is law. His wish is his family's command. It has been this way for countless centuries. In a land where honor and respect are so important, this tradition is woven into the very fabric of everyday life. Joon Chul Pak wanted his second daughter, Se Ri, to become a great golfer. He knew she had a special athletic gift, and believed he could transform her into a champion in the game he loved. There were, however, some obstacles.

First of all, Se Ri seemed to have little interest in golf. In elementary school, she excelled in track and field, and by her teen years was an accomplished sprinter, hurdler, and shot-putter. Joon Chul was an excellent amateur golfer, and practiced as often as he could. One day, when Se Ri was a fourth grader, her father took her with him while he worked on his chip shots. After a while, she asked if she could try. Se Ri grabbed a club and mimicked her dad's swing perfectly. Within a half hour, she was able to place the ball wherever she wanted. Despite this initial success, however, Se Ri did not pursue golf seriously for several more years.

Se Ri showed a natural flair for golf from the age of 11, and began winning small trophies at local amateur events at the age of 14. The tournaments—and trophies—have been getting bigger ever since.

Another problem the Paks faced was that there was no place for Se Ri to learn the game. There was only one public course in all of South Korea, where golf was (and for the most part, still is) a game for the very wealthy. The cost of joining a private country club can be hundreds of thousands of dollars. Joon Chul did not make that kind of money at his job.

Did You Know?

Once Se Ri got interested in golf, she played every day, regardless of the weather. She worked in the blistering heat of summer and the bleakness of winter. Sometimes, it got so cold that icicles would form in her hair.

Actually, no one was quite sure what his job was, or where his money came from. He operated on the fringes of the hotel and construction industries, supplying sand and pebbles for building projects. It was suspected that he had ties to organized crime. When Se Ri was young, Joon Chul actually had to move his family to Hawaii to live with his mother for several months while the South Korean government was rounding up gangsters in the Paks' hometown of Daejeon. When the sweep ended, he moved back. During an argument with two former partners, Joon Chul was stabbed 17 times. Today, he describes himself as having been a "thug," but will say no more.

Joon Chul Pak might have had the talent to become a professional golfer—he even won a few tournaments—but he did not have the patience or inner balance you need to play well week after week. Se Ri's mother, Jeong Sook, had more than enough of both. She taught her three daughters to step back from a situation and view it calmly

Se Ri's mother, Jeong Sook (left), taught her lessons that helped in golf, and in life.

It's Been Done
BEFORE

What kind of golfer can you create from someone whose best sports were sprinting, hurdling, and shot-putting? A great one! In the 1930s, America's top track and field athlete was Mildred "Babe" Didrikson. She won three Olympic medals and excelled in the same events as Se Ri. A few years later, she began playing golf, and became the greatest female player ever. In fact, she was one of the founders of the Ladies Professional Golf Association (LPGA)!

and rationally before acting or forming an opinion. This helped her deal with her husband during some rough spots in their marriage, and imbued Se Ri with tremendous poise and confidence.

Se Ri's father knew that she would play golf if he ordered her to, but he also understood that she would never develop his love for the game if he forced her into it. So he waited. Finally, when she was 14, he took her to a local junior tournament. He hoped that the beautiful setting of a golf club would capture her imagination. The strategy worked. "I saw all the green grass, the fresh air, the people dressed well," remembers Se Ri. "I decided I wanted to change."

Realizing she was way behind other golfers her age, Se Ri began practicing as much as she could—often six hours or more a day. Her dad explained to her that she would have to do more than practice. To reach the sport's highest level, she would have to be in great condition. He would wake her up at 5:30 in the morning and make her run up and down the steps of their 15-story apartment building.

After Se Ri dedicated herself to golf, she and her father,
Joon Chul, were inseparable both on and off the course.

Joon Chul also told Se Ri that she would not succeed unless she was mentally tough. He whacked her with a stick called a *pechori* whenever she made a bad shot, and played all sorts of mind games to try and break her concentration. "He was pushing me, pushing me to be better, and I knew that," Se Ri claims. "I wanted to make him and my mother proud. And then I began to love golf."

The lessons continued even when Se Ri did not have a club in her hands. Joon Chul once took her to watch pit bulls fight. Se Ri agreed to go because she loved dogs and was concerned that they were being hurt. What she saw horrified her. It was a wild battle between two flesh-ripping, bone-crunching animals, with people cheering and laughing and betting on the outcome. She left shaken, but got the point: Golf may be a game, but survival is a very serious, sometimes ugly business.

Joon Chul also said Se Ri would not be a champion until she was totally fearless. One day, he asked her what scared her most. "Cemeteries," she answered. She soon found herself practicing in a vacant lot down the street, right next to a graveyard. Later, her father pitched a tent inside the cemetery and they spent the night. Eventually, Se Ri's dad had her stay in the tent by herself. "Sometimes it got scary," she says. "Especially when it got really dark, and I had to walk home alone."

KNOW THE SCORE

In golf, a player must complete a hole in a certain number of shots. On a typical hole—a "par 4"—a player gets four strokes. A short hole is usually a "par 3," while a long hole is sometimes a "par 5." If a player rolls the ball into the hole in one less shot than par, it is called a "birdie." If a player takes one shot too many, it is called a "bogey." A round of golf is always 18 holes, and par for a round is usually in the neighborhood of 72 strokes, depending on the makeup of the course. At the end of a tournament, the player who finishes with the lowest score is declared the winner.

After practicing shots next to a cemetery, nothing fazes Se Ri anymore.

Pak Attack

chapter 1

*"I stayed with golf in the begin-
ning because I wanted to prove
to people that he wasn't crazy."*
— SE RI PAK

Se Ri had played only a handful of rounds on an actual golf course when she entered her first junior event, at the age of 14. The Lyle and Scott Tournament was held in the capital city of Seoul, a couple of hours from her home. She and her dad drove there, surveyed the course, sized up the competition, and discussed how she could win. Se Ri then went out and executed their plan to perfection. And she won!

Encouraged by this wonderful start, Joon Chul scraped together $200,000 and bought a membership at a country club so Se Ri could practice on a real course whenever she wanted. It nearly bankrupted the family, and after a year it became clear that he could not afford the annual fees. But in that year Se Ri made terrific progress, especially on her drives and approach shots. She also became quite adept at putting with an unorthodox cross-handed grip. After the club membership ran out, Se Ri literally did her learning during tournaments. She would experiment and make mistakes in the first round, then try to apply what she had learned in the final round.

*Se Ri displays the cross-handed putting grip her father taught her.
She is one of the few pros who use this unorthodox style.*

When Se Ri was 15, she entered the prestigious Golf Digest Cup in Yeo Ju City. Most of the other girls in the tournament had wealthy parents and played every weekend at country clubs. When Joon Chul approached some of the other moms and dads prior to tee-off, they ignored him. Infuriated by this snub, he yelled for Se Ri to come to where the winner's cup was on display. "Here," he said, handing the trophy to his daughter, "this is yours." Se Ri's father told everyone that she had every right to hold it, because she was going to win it anyway. Se Ri just nodded. A few days later the trophy was sitting on a shelf in the Pak home.

Incredibly, Se Ri won more than 30 amateur events over a four-year span. During Se Ri's rise to prominence, her father decided that he had better devote his full time to her career. He turned over the running of his company to Se Ri's mom, spent thousands of dollars on the best golf equipment available, and invested what was left of the

"Her emotions are not part of the mix. Controlling your emotions, not being open about your emotions—Asian culture views this as a strength."

JUDY RANKIN, TV COMMENTATOR

family's savings in travel to tournaments beyond South Korea.

Se Ri began to experience a different kind of pressure than what she had felt on the golf course. Her father was now her constant companion, from five in the morning until eleven at night. During practice, Joon Chul would berate Se Ri when she hit a bad shot. When she told him she wished she had more friends, he told her to forget it; *he* was her friend. If she went to the movies, he went with her. If she went shopping, he was there, too. Of course, Se Ri was just as tough on herself. If she hit a bad shot in a tournament—even if she *won* the tournament—she would stay afterwards and hit that same shot over and over until she got it right.

Meanwhile, the family construction business was sputtering. The money was not coming in at the rate it once had and Se Ri's mom had to work a second job, as a cook in a karaoke bar. Now everyone in the Pak family was depending on Se Ri to make it. Her mother was not convinced Joon Chul was handling things correctly, and they would debate the issue into the night. She was concerned for the welfare of her children, and especially worried that Se Ri was being pushed far too hard. "She's going to die," Jeong Sook once warned him.

Sometimes, it was all too much for Se Ri. "I was really upset many times because I just wanted my dad to give me more rest," she says. "But he didn't do that. Many, many times I cried. But then I thought, 'Show your dad you can do it—you can do anything if you want.'"

amateur *achiever*

Se Ri was the Korean High School Champion from 1993 to 1995, and the Korean Open Champion in 1992 and 1996. In 1994 she finished third at the World Amateur Championship in France.

In 1995, Joon Chul felt that Se Ri was ready to play big competitions outside of South Korea. The two traveled to the United States for the U.S. Amateur Championship. Se Ri made it all the way to the semifinals, where she lost in match play to Kelli Kuehne, one of the rising stars on the world amateur scene. Se Ri's performance opened a lot of eyes. By the conclusion of the tournament, she too was being considered one of the sport's top young golfers.

It was also around this time that Se Ri discovered her first hero. "When I was 17, I was watching a women's tournament at home and saw Nancy Lopez. She was always smiling and seemed to be having a good time. And I decided then I wanted to be like her."

In April 1996, Se Ri officially turned professional. She entered 14 South Korean LPGA events and did sensationally. She finished first or second in all but one tournament, and became her country's second-biggest sports star, behind baseball pitcher Chan Ho Park. President Kim Dae Jung declared her a "national hero."

Se Ri was something special. She was never nervous, never even flustered. She seemed to thrive on pressure when other players fell apart. By the end of 1996, Se Ri was thinking about playing in the United States on the LPGA Tour. She did not know much about American golf or American golfers, but she knew she had to beat the best to be the best. By her 18th birthday, Se Ri set quite a goal for herself. "I wanted to become the finest female golfer in the world."

Before Se Ri came along, Chan Ho Park of the Los Angeles Dodgers was South Korea's most famous athlete. Today, both are considered national treasures.

Swinging Into School

"After watching her swing a few times, I knew she was the real thing."

— COACH DAVID LEADBETTER

Many in South Korea shared Se Ri's dream. Among her fans were the executives of Samsung, one of the country's largest corporations. Samsung makes home electronics, cars, airplanes, chemicals, watches, golf equipment, and sells life insurance, and stocks and bonds. In order to gain greater recognition outside of Asia, the company needed an international celebrity who could draw attention to the many things it does. In December 1996, Samsung decided that Se Ri had a chance of becoming that shining star.

The company agreed to sponsor Se Ri and send her to the United States. It guaranteed a good annual salary, reimbursement for expenses, and generous bonuses if she did well. Se Ri also received a large signing bonus, which was a great help to her family. Things had gotten so bad that she

Did You Know?

David Leadbetter put Se Ri on a rigorous fitness program, and a strict dietary regimen to make her leaner and give her more endurance. The first time he saw her tear into a pizza, he knew he had better limit her fast-food intake!

was taking public buses to many of her tournaments, and Joon Chul had been hospitalized with an ulcer. The agreement covered 10 years, and involved more money than any deal of its kind in women's golf. Samsung told Se Ri she would have the best of everything, that all of her needs would be seen to, and that she would be free to concentrate on nothing but golf.

To protect its investment, Samsung assigned a team of executives to handle Se Ri both in South Korea and the United States. A 28-year-old former sportswriter, Steven Kil, was given the task of being Se Ri's interpreter, secretary, and press agent. The two would share a large condominium at the Lake Nona Golf Club, in Orlando, Florida.

Se Ri swings for a group of her fans in Seoul, South Korea, at one of many events in which she has participated for her sponsor, Samsung.

Why Orlando? Because that is where one of the top golf teachers in the world is headquartered. His name is David Leadbetter, and Samsung wrote him a check for more than $100,000 to work with Se Ri and sharpen her game. Although Leadbetter had worked with female golfers from time to time, he had never taken one on as a full-time pupil. Once he saw Se Ri's swing, however, he had no doubt he could help her.

When coach David Leadbetter first saw Se Ri's powerful style, he compared it to a man's swing.

She had big muscles around her midsection, which meant she could generate great club speed without using her legs, arms, and wrists. Getting these three parts of the body to work in concert is difficult, particularly when they must supply a golfer's power. Some young players take five to 10 years before they get everything working together consistently. Se Ri's swing was different. It was more like a man's—more like the swings Leadbetter had made his reputation fine-tuning.

Indeed, some would say her swing comes right out of the PGA textbook—especially the way her right shoulder rotates so far forward toward her target. Se Ri possessed remarkable strength and flexibility, which are the keys to hitting long and hard.

They got to work immediately. Leadbetter broke down Se Ri's swing component by component and began building it back up again. He spent four to six hours a day with Se Ri. He loved the fact that she was always willing to put in more time. It had been the same way with his most famous pupil, Nick Faldo, a legendary hard worker.

Some of the initial adjustments Leadbetter made focused on the differences between the way golf is taught in Asia and the United States. Golfers on the other side of the Pacific tend to stand far from the ball, and compensate by bending forward. This produces a little extra power, but can lead to inconsistency. Leadbetter moved Se Ri closer to the ball. She did not need the extra body torque—her legs and midsection would supply all the power she needed.

Another area on which Leadbetter worked was Se Ri's putting. In South Korea, most greens have Korai grass, which has thicker blades and slows the ball down. In the United States, the grass is much finer and the greens much faster. When she first came to the United States, her putts were too strong, usually rolling past the hole. Se Ri had to relearn how to "read" greens and also adjust her approach shots so they would not bounce past the pin.

Although Se Ri was pleased with her progress, she was not happy about living so far from home. Steven Kil was a nice man, but he was much older—and technically her employee. Se Ri had no one her own age with whom she could hang around, talk, or have fun. She also missed her family. She ran up tremendous phone bills, calling them every day. At night, she mostly listened to her language tapes. When Se Ri arrived in the United States, she only knew a couple of words of English, but within a few months she begun to understand and speak the language enough to carry on a short conversation.

> **Did You Know?**
>
> In most tournaments, the field is cut down after two days, with only the top players allowed to continue on. In her six LPGA appearances in 1997, Se Ri made the cut five times.

Occasionally, Leadbetter would send Se Ri out to play an event. In 1997 she participated in six LPGA tournaments, including the U.S. Women's Open in July. Se Ri finished a very respectable 21st, and got to meet Nancy Lopez for the first time. Se Ri also returned to South Korea for a couple of tournaments. It was great to see her family again, and the fans gave her a warm welcome. Se Ri responded by winning both events, edging Kelli Kuehne in the Rose Open, and dominating at the Seoul Open with a nine-stroke victory over Laura Davies. As good as Se Ri had been before she left for the United States, she was now far better.

Among David Leadbetter's most famous successes were Greg Norman, Ernie Els, and Nick Faldo, three of the greatest players ever. Leadbetter's work with Faldo (left) was legendary; it was said he "remade" the Englishman's swing.

Se Ri had her "game face" on for the final round of the 1997 LPGA qualifying tournament. People are still talking about her magnificent run that day on the back nine.

The final leg of Se Ri's 1997 adventure was the LPGA's Qualifying Tournament, or "Q-School," as the players call it. At the end of each year, a tournament is held to determine which up-and-coming golfers are good enough to earn a Tour Card, which enables them to enter the following year's LPGA events. About three dozen players get their cards, and competition is fierce. Some players try again and again, for years, without ever getting cards. The tournament was held at the LPGA International Golf Club in Daytona Beach, Florida—not far from Orlando. Leadbetter sent one of his most trusted assistants, Tom Creavy, to serve as Se Ri's caddie. There was little doubt that she would earn her card, but he was not taking chances.

Se Ri shot a sparkling 68 the first day, but followed it with a sloppy 76 in the second round. Following a bad day with a good one is the mark of a pro. In the third round, Se Ri went out and looked like she did not even remember the 76. She whipped through the course with a 67 to put her among the leaders and assure her of her card. On the final day, Se Ri started well and made her pars. But she was still six strokes behind the leader, Cristie Kerr, with just 10 holes left to play. At this point, there was no money at stake, and little prestige in winning the event, so no one expected Se Ri to try to make up the difference. That is because no one knew Se Ri.

The golf world got a glimpse of its own future on the back nine that day. Se Ri got aggressive and nailed six birdies in rapid succession. By the time she reached the green on 18, she was in a position to sink a putt for her seventh birdie and a most miraculous victory. She could have killed herself when she rimmed a 5-footer (1.5 m) to end up in a tie. Still, her 10-under par score established a new record for the tournament.

When Se Ri tapped the ball in, the game face disappeared and a teenager's face shone out from under her visor. She broke into a wide smile when she saw Kuehne, and the two young stars celebrated their new status as LPGA pros with a big high five.

"When I played golf in Korea, every time I won, or was second. Here, it's not easy. It's difficult here. There are many strong players."
SE RI PAK

Major Mover

"I saw her play golf in Asia when she was just 16 and I said to myself at the time that if this kid ever gets to the LPGA, I want to be on her bag."

— TREE CABLE

Everyone in golf seemed to have an opinion on how Se Ri would do in her first year on the pro tour. Some predicted she would make as big a splash as Karrie Webb had in 1996, when she finished second on the prize-money list during her rookie season. Others cautioned that, despite Se Ri's obvious talents, it might take her time to get used to life on the LPGA Tour. David Leadbetter thought his prize student had a chance to win one or two tournaments during 1998. He knew when Se Ri got really "locked in," she could put together four rounds as good as anyone on the tour. Se Ri predicted she would win five tournaments, which happened to be more than any rookie since—who else?—Nancy Lopez, who captured nine in 1978.

Se Ri spent the first few months of 1998 getting used to her new schedule. Most players on the LPGA Tour arrive at a typical tournament on Monday, shoot a practice round on Tuesday, play in a pro-amateur event on Wednesday, then get down to business on Thursday. After two rounds, if they have made the cut, they play two more, taking them through Sunday. Then it starts all over again the following week. Participating in two consecutive tournaments is pretty exhausting; after three in a row, a golfer's brain turns to mush. Anything past that is considered foolish.

Se Ri did not know this. She was unaccustomed to taking a week off. She did not even like to take a *day* off. So when other golfers were relaxing, she was either entered in a tournament or—if there was not one scheduled—practicing her rear end off in preparation for the next event. After one tournament, she went right from the 18th hole back to the first tee, and played another round. Se Ri also was unaccustomed to not winning. After the season's fourth tournament, she asked her caddy, Tree Cable, why she hadn't won yet!

Heading into her first "major" of 1998, Se Ri stood 45th in the rankings. Her best showing to

Se Ri's caddie, Jeff "Tree" Cable, comes by his nickname honestly.

that point had come in April, at the Longs Drug Challenge, where she finished 11th. At the prestigious LPGA Championship, Se Ri was expected to hold her own, but was not yet considered a serious threat to challenge the leaders. On this course, in particular, it seemed unlikely that a rookie would do well. The DuPont Country Club is unforgiving, with deep rough and narrow fairways. Also working against Se Ri was the weather, which limited her practice time at DuPont. In fact, when the tournament started, she had not even seen all 18 holes—Se Ri would be playing the back nine "blind."

On the first hole of the tournament, Se Ri scored a birdie. She kept on rolling from there, out-driving and out-putting the rest of the field for a magnificent 65. The fairways were still damp, which prevented tee shots from rolling very far

> ## Did You Know?
>
> *The last rookie to score her first LPGA victory in a major tournament was Liselotte Neumann, who won the U.S. Open in 1988. At 20, Se Ri was the youngest player to win a major since Sandra Post won the LPGA Championship in 1968.*

once they hit the ground. That made it impossible for most of the others to do much more than try for par on the long par-five holes. But because Se Ri hit the ball so high and so far, 250 to 275 yards (228 to 251 m), she was able to score birdies. She birdied all three par-5s, playing the course as if she had designed it herself. Her approach shots

were spectacular, too. On 7, Se Ri smashed a long five iron to within a foot (30 cm) of the cup. On 11, she chipped to just 3 feet (90 cm) away. She finished the day at six under par, with a one-stroke lead over Lisa Walters. The next morning, every newspaper in South Korea had Se Ri's picture on the front page.

On the tournament's second day, Se Ri erased any doubts about rookie jitters when she birdied two of the first three holes and whittled another stroke off her score later in the round to finish with a 3-under-par 68. She now led Walters by two strokes and Lisa Hackney, the LPGA's 1997 Rookie of the Year, by three.

Se Ri's game was supersharp at the LPGA Championship, as she zeroed in on her first professional victory.

> *"As long as she enjoys being out there—and it looks like she does—she'll be a strong player for a long time."*
>
> LISA HACKNEY—WITH SE RI AFTER THE JAMIE FARR KROGER CLASSIC

Nancy Lopez, who played with Se Ri during the first two rounds, marveled at her composure. The 20-year-old stroked her par-saving shots with the same coolness as her birdie attempts. And when she needed to land a difficult shot, she was absolutely fearless. It reminded Lopez of herself at the same age.

As the third day began, everyone watched to see if Se Ri would fold under the pressure of being the Saturday morning leader. On the third hole, she pulled her tee shot into the water, producing a lot of knowing nods in the gallery. This would be the beginning of the end, many thought. But after taking a penalty stroke and dropping a new ball on the grass, Se Ri drew a deep breath, grabbed a five wood out of her bag and belted a wondrous 195-yard (178-m) drive that rolled to within a few feet of the pin. The stunned crowd erupted into thunderous applause. Instead of a bogey or double-bogey, she emerged from her first bad hole of the tournament with a par. This kid was all right!

Over the next dozen holes, Se Ri's game continued to click. And although she missed a couple of birdie putts, she

Did You Know?

When Se Ri returned to her hotel room after the third round of the LPGA Championship, she got a call from David Leadbetter. He had watched her on TV and noticed a slight flaw. Shorten up on your putting stroke, he told her, and you'll be fine. The next day she putted beautifully and won tho tournament.

made her pars and continued to lead the tournament. Only on 17, when she muffed an easy putt, did she lose sole possession of first place, falling into a tie with Hackney, who was also playing well. Se Ri finished the day with a nifty putt for par on 18, illustrating again how well she bounced back from adversity. "I forgot about the short putt,"

Se Ri became the first rookie in a decade to win a major when she held on to her lead at the LPGA Championship.

she says of the nerve-jangling bogey on 17. "I didn't mind because I had another hole. It's not the way I think."

Despite Se Ri's magnificent performance, few veteran observers believed she could hold on for the final round. There was just too much fire power behind her. But Se Ri played tough, made her shots, and began to pull away from the field after the 13th hole. She made a par-saving approach shot on 14 and a tough, 20-foot birdie putt on 15. Hackney watched in awe as Se Ri belted a long tee shot on the par-5 16th hole, then reached the green with her next shot. Two putts later, she was up three strokes and never looked back.

Not once did Se Ri appear nervous. Nor did she even seem to know the score. In fact, the gravity of her achievement—a rookie winning the LPGA Championship!—never entered her mind. "I didn't think about if I would win," she says. "I just played my game."

Se Ri shows off her first trophy as an LPGA pro. Those who predicted she would falter on the final day learned that she could "close out" a tournament like a tour veteran.

Se Ri and Tree ponder a tricky shot from the rough during the third round of the 1998 U.S. Open. It was the most difficult round of her life, yet she managed to finish the day one stroke up.

Hotter Than July

chapter 5

"To win two majors your rookie year is really something."

— KARRIE WEBB, LPGA STAR

ack in South Korea, Se Ri's victory touched off a wild predawn celebration. Already the most popular female athlete in her country, she had become a national treasure. Poor Steven Kil had to deal with hundreds of letters, faxes, and phone calls from her family, friends, and fans, not to mention the folks at Samsung. Thousands of Korean girls suddenly wanted to start playing golf. And everyone was calling Se Ri the "female Tiger Woods." It was an honor, of course, but the more she thought about the comparison, the more it rubbed her the wrong way. "Every time I hear Tiger Woods first and me second," she says, "I want it me first, then later Tiger!"

The next stop on the tour was the U.S. Women's Open, in Kohler, Wisconsin. Back when Se Ri and her father had begun setting goals for her career, they agreed that she would be ready to win her first major by the age of 26 or 27. Now here she was, at the age of 20, with a chance to win her second major in a row!

This would not be an easy accomplishment. The site of the '98 Open, Blackwolf Run, is one of the most difficult courses ever designed. Experts agreed that this would

be the perfect opportunity for Se Ri to establish herself on tour. There was no "out-muscling" this course. It required finesse, intelligence, and nerves of steel—a few bad holes in a row, and you're out of the tournament.

Se Ri battled the course to a standoff the first day, finishing with a 69. In a second round plagued by rain and lightning, she finished with a 70, which was good enough to put her atop the leader board. Day three brought treacherous wind gusts, and presented Se Ri with the most challenging round of her short career. No one in the tournament broke par, but Se Ri held her own to maintain a one-stroke lead. Meanwhile, many of the LPGA's big names got swept right off the course. Those who remained in the hunt on Sunday were mentally and physically exhausted. It had been three rounds of sheer misery.

> ## Did You Know?
>
> To reward herself for her LPGA Championship win—and battle the loneliness that comes with having no friends her age on the tour—Se Ri purchased a five-week-old beagle puppy and named it Happy.

Se Ri knew winning would come down to surviving, and this she did, shooting a 76. The veterans, meanwhile, all ran out of gas by the end of the day. This allowed an unknown 20-year-old amateur from Duke University named Jenny Chuasiriporn to creep up the leader board. Playing in the group ahead of Se Ri, she drew within a single stroke of the lead, and on the 18th hole drilled an impossible 45-foot (13-m) birdie putt to earn a tie.

Se Ri, standing on the 18th tee waiting to play, heard the crowd roar. She had just bogeyed 17, and knew it would now take a birdie on 18 to win. Two solid shots got her to within 10 feet (3 m) of the pin, but she failed to hole her third shot. Incredibly, after four grueling days, the U.S. Open was tied. The two young ladies would have to play 18 more holes on Monday to determine the 1998 champion.

The pressure was on Se Ri the next morning, and she knew it. Chuasiriporn was an amateur whom no one expected to win, and thus she had nothing to lose. Se Ri, on the other hand, had to prove she was for real—that she could stand up to a challenge. At first, it looked as if things would not be going Se Ri's way. She bogeyed the third hole, while Chuasiriporn birdied three of the first five. Down four strokes with just 13 holes left, Se Ri just concentrated on playing her game and hoped that her opponent would

Se Ri acknowledges the crowd's applause after her putt on 18 at the U.S. Open, which tied her with Jenny Chuasiriporn. The two continued their dramatic battle the following day.

Se Ri had to play catch-up during the playoff round of the 1998 U.S. Open, as Jenny Chuasiriporn made birdies on three of the first five holes.

make a few mistakes. Over the next seven holes, that is exactly what happened. Se Ri remained within striking distance and then birdied 11 and 12 to pull even.

The two were still tied when they stepped to the 18th tee. Chuasiriporn ripped a beauty right down the fairway. Astonishingly, Se Ri hooked her shot to the left. The ball rolled down an embankment and into a pond. Most players would have folded at this point, but Se Ri took things in stride. "You can't always have a good bounce," she says. "Sometimes you get a bad lie. Now it was time to try something new."

Se Ri had a choice. She could play it safe, take a one-shot penalty, and drop the ball on the bank. Or she could try to hit the ball underwater, lob it over the 6-foot (2-m) bank, and get into position on the fairway for a long approach shot. Se Ri decided to go for broke. She removed her shoes, peeled off her socks, and waded calf-deep in the water. She had practiced a lot of weird shots in her

Se Ri jumps into her father's arms after sinking the winning putt at the U.S. Open. It was the first time her parents had attended one of her tournaments in the United States.

Golf's young guns embrace after playing a record 92 holes. Se Ri and Jenny Chuasiriporn should give LPGA fans plenty to cheer about in the years to come.

life, but never one quite like this. Se Ri drew her club back, brought it down into the water as hard as she could, and blasted the ball back into play. It was one of the great shots of the year. Her next shot made the green, and she two-putted for a bogey five.

Chuasiriporn, meanwhile, was on the fringe of the green in two. She simply needed to get close with her first putt, then roll in her second for the championship. Suddenly, her hands started to shake. Moments later, she missed the easy tournament-winner. After 90 holes the two were tied again!

Now came sudden death; the first player to win a hole would be crowned U.S. Open champion. Never before in the history of the event had things gone so far. The first hole was a long par 5, which both players parred. The second hole of sudden death was a shorter par 4. Both players reached the green in two shots. Chuasiriporn missed her birdie try from 18 feet (5 m). Pak's third shot, also from 18 feet, rolled right into the cup for the victory. When she looked up and saw her parents, she burst into tears. Se Ri knew she had made it. She was the best.

Did You Know?

Se Ri says big crowds like the one at the U.S. Open actually help her. "It makes my game stronger— it makes me want to show the fans a great shot."

Se Ri
Confidential

Whenever fans ask Se Ri for advice, she tries to pass on the lessons her parents taught her.

"It's important to be strong, but golf is not about strength. The secret to the golf swing is tempo and rhythm."

"I had good mental training. Think the way my father taught me: Attack the course."

"I just practice, sleep, eat, practice."

"My dad wanted to teach me how to control myself. Now it's automatic. I can do it myself."

The Korean Express

chapter 6

"She never gets ahead of herself.
Each shot is like the only shot
of the day for her."

— MEG MALLON, LPGA STAR

Se Ri won twice more that July. After the U.S. Open, Samsung flew her by private jet to the Jamie Farr Classic in Ohio. After 92 holes of golf the week before, she was exhausted—and it showed in the first round, as she played sloppy golf for the first time all year. Unfazed, Se Ri got 10 hours' sleep, then went out and shot the best round in the history of women's golf.

She completed 18 holes in 61 shots, making 10 birdies, no bogeys, and reading the greens flawlessly. On the last hole, she rolled in a dramatic 20-footer (6 m) for the record. "I felt like I could make anything," she remembers of that second round. "Every putt was perfect, right to left and left to right."

Se Ri's record-setting performance put her into the lead by two strokes heading into the weekend. On Saturday, she continued to scorch the ball, shooting a 63 to open up an insurmountable nine-shot lead over Karrie Webb. Again, Se Ri made 10 birdies. On the final day, she shot a 66 for a four-day total of 261, which obliterated the lowest score in LPGA history for a tournament. She finished 23 strokes under par, which tied a tour record. On 18, she needed to sink an 18-foot putt to go 24-under, but came up a foot short. The crowd groaned when the ball stopped rolling, but Se Ri just smiled. She tapped the ball in, hugged Webb and Tree Cable, and then tossed the ball into the crowd, nearly starting a riot.

The final stop for the LPGA tour in July was the Giant Eagle LPGA Classic, also in Ohio. Se Ri played well in the early going, staying close to the leaders, and making just one

Se Ri continues her magical season at the Jamie Farr Classic. Her 10-under-par 61 established a new record for the best round in LPGA history.

bogey during the entire tournament. At the beginning of the final round, she was only three shots behind Dottie Pepper. Pepper hit her first drive into a lake for a double-bogey, and soon found herself a shot behind Se Ri. The two jockeyed for position the rest of the way, with Pepper pulling even on the 17th hole with a 5-foot (1.5-m) birdie.

Se Ri, playing in the group ahead of Pepper, responded to this challenge with a long drive off the tee on the par-5 18th. She hit a beautiful second shot which carried all the way to the lip of the green, then trickled to within 15 feet (4.5 m) of the cup. As Pepper walked down the fairway after *her* tee shot on 18, she watched as Se Ri missed her 15-foot putt by a couple of inches. It never occurred to her that Se Ri had gotten to the green in just two strokes, so when she tapped in the ball for a birdie four, Pepper assumed she had just completed her fifth shot.

Before Se Ri's final putt on 18, Meg Mallon (right) offered her red-hot playing partner her putter, as if to say, "Here, maybe you'll have better luck with this." The gallery erupted in laughter. Even Se Ri, game face and all, had to smile at that one.

Pepper nearly made an eagle herself on 18, but her putt rolled past the cup, stopping 4 feet (1.2 m) beyond the hole. Mistakingly thinking that her next putt would win the tournament, she lined up the four-footer and barely missed. Disappointed but not devastated, Pepper tapped in and reached into the hole to pull out her ball, readying herself for a playoff with Se Ri. But when she looked up and saw her caddie pull off his identification bib, she knew something was terribly wrong. Se Ri was the winner.

Se Ri credits this victory—her third in four tournaments—to something Nancy Lopez had told her. The two had become close during the summer, and Se Ri thought of Nancy as kind of a second mother. At the beginning of the tournament, Lopez told Se Ri that it looked like something was troubling her. Se Ri responded that she was worried about her schedule. She had already committed to play five events in a row and was feeling pressure to play two more on top of that. She also was having a hard time relaxing, she told Lopez.

The veteran's response was that she was 20, she was a rookie, and that she did not have to play any tournament she did not want to. It was good to hear someone say that. Se Ri relaxed, played great golf, and won. Then she began to think about taking some time off.

The Pak File

SE RI'S FAVORITE...

Athlete	Nancy Lopez
Actors	Sean Connery & Jackie Chan
Movie	*Titanic*
Food	Coconut shrimp
Flavor	Chocolate
Travel Companion	Teddy bear
Cartoon Characters	Bugs Bunny & Tom and Jerry
Video Game	Mortal Kombat
Cable Channel	The Disney Channel
Car	Mercedes SUV

SE RI'S SECRET AMBITION:
"If I come back in this world, I want to come back as a man...and be the best player on the men's tour!"

Did You Know?

Only three players in history have won the tournament right after they won the U.S. Open. The first was the legendary Louise Suggs, in 1952.

Wearing Out

chapter 7

"When does Se Ri have time for Se Ri?"
— LORIE KANE, LPGA STAR

A week later, Se Ri entered the du Maurier Classic, her fifth event in five weeks. It was quite a scene. Nearly 1,000 Koreans made their way to the city of Windsor, in the Canadian province of Ontario. They wanted to see if Se Ri could become the first player since Pat Bradley in 1986 to win three majors in the same year. The media crush was unprecedented. More than 500 sets of press credentials were issued for the tournament—triple the normal amount in years past. About a sixth of that number consisted of reporters, photographers, and television crews from South Korea. LPGA officials loved that Se Ri's popularity had mushroomed so quickly, but at the du Maurier they were unprepared to handle the media circus that now surrounded her every move.

Did You Know?

Se Ri believes that male and female golfers should get equal respect. "People say PGA first, then LPGA—like it's a little behind. I don't like that. We're all professionals."

Meeting the demands of reporters, photographers, and television crews is now a fact of life for Se Ri. She has learned that being one of the world's best players can have its drawbacks.

The phone in Se Ri's hotel room rang constantly. Directors from other tournaments followed her everywhere, hoping to get her to commit to playing their events in 1999. People representing charities begged her to make appearances or donations. And everyone wanted her for an "exclusive" one-on-one interview. Afterwards Steven Kil figured that, had Se Ri honored every interview request while she was there, she would have had to skip the tournament!

Se Ri did not win the du Maurier, nor any other tournaments, during the final weeks of the 1998 season. She was exhausted. She played her remaining events mostly on sheer will and adrenaline. Everything Se Ri had wanted as a pro had come to her in

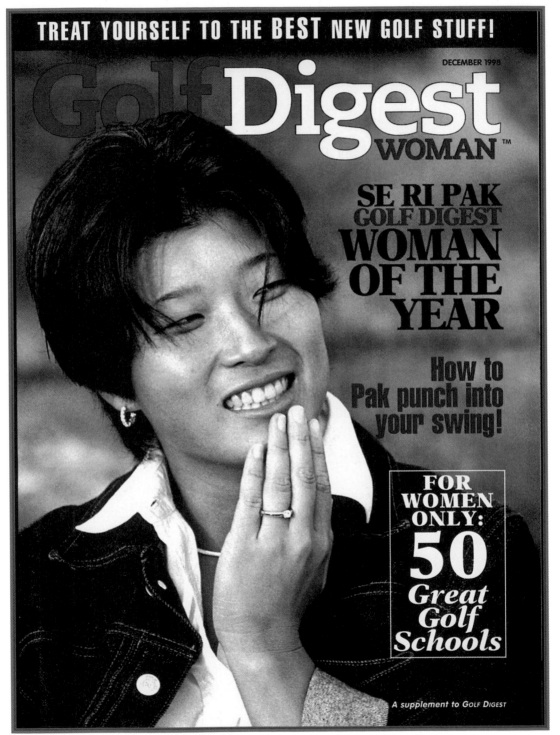

When Se Ri began the 1998 season, few fans outside of South Korea had ever heard of her. Now she regularly graces the covers of the sport's top magazines.

such a short time; she was beginning to see that instant celebrity was not all it is cracked up to be. "Things happened so fast," she laments. "I was just looking to learn the golf courses the first few years."

Se Ri had become the most recognized player in women's golf, and people in the LPGA were suddenly counting on her to carry the sport forward. She wanted very much to do this, and agreed to try just about anything the association asked. She knew the women's game had a long way to go (women make less than half what their male counterparts make) and that she could help broaden its market appeal. But when, Se Ri wondered, is it all right to say NO?

In September, as the LPGA season wound down, Se Ri began to look

An exhausted Se Ri waves goodbye to South Korean fans after her October 1998 "victory tour."

at her world with a more critical eye. Her first decision was to have Steven Kil replaced. Although the two had become friends, Steven worked for Samsung and the requests he was delivering from the company were becoming increasingly infuriating to Se Ri. She understood that she had obligations under the terms of their endorsement deal—and

"By winning four LPGA tournaments at a time that the nation was suffering difficult times, Pak encouraged the Korean people to have confidence that they can overcome the crisis."

PRIME MINISTER KIM JONG PIL (LEFT, SHAKING HANDS WITH KIM DAE JUNG)

that Steven was caught in an impossible situation—but someone had to set some limits on these requests, and Steven was not in a position to do so.

That October, Se Ri returned to South Korea for what should have been an unprecedented victory celebration. She had left the country alone a year earlier, with a set of clubs, some luggage, and her hopes and dreams. She returned clutching a teddy bear and a bouquet of flowers—followed by an entourage of 30, including LPGA officials, golf writers, and her caddie.

In a country struggling through a financial recession (its worse in four decades) Se Ri's presence promised to lift everyone's spirits. But in the middle of a whirlwind schedule of speeches, public appearances, and closed-door meetings, Se Ri collapsed. The next thing she knew, she was in a hospital bed.

professional *stats*

Year	Event	Cuts Made	Birdies	Eagles	Per Round Average	Top 10 Finishes	Wins	Prize Money
1998	27	26*	337**	2	71.4	8	4***	$872,140****

* Tied for third on LPGA tour   ** Fourth on LPGA tour
*** Tied for first on LPGA tour   **** Second on LPGA tour

achievements

- U.S. Women's Open winner
- Youngest winner of U.S. Women's Open
- Lowest score for an LPGA tournament
- LPGA Championship winner
- Best round in LPGA history
- LPGA Rookie of the Year

The final tally on her unprecedented rookie year was four wins, including two majors, and $872,170.00 in prize money, placing her second to Annika Sorenstam.

Whose Life Is It Anyway?

chapter 8

"What's happening now definitely reminds me of what was happening to me."

— NANCY LOPEZ

At the beginning of 1998, Se Ri was a kid. By the end of the year, she was a "commodity." Everyone, it seemed, wanted a piece of Se Ri Pak. Unfortunately, there just was not enough to go around. She knew that her career was out of control. The problem was, she had never really learned how to stand up for herself. She had no idea what to do next.

Se Ri still looked to her father for advice, but Joon Chul had taken her as far as he could. At this point, he knew even less about the world of professional golf than his daughter. Several agents approached the family, explaining that Se Ri would need experienced representation to navigate the complex waters ahead. This

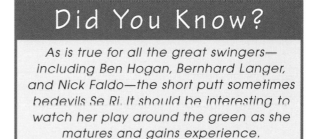

Did You Know?

As is true for all the great swingers—including Ben Hogan, Bernhard Langer, and Nick Faldo—the short putt sometimes bedevils Se Ri. It should be interesting to watch her play around the green as she matures and gains experience.

sounded like a good idea—someone needed to handle the details of her life and decide what she could and could not do. The search began.

Se Ri's meeting with Tiger Woods and coach Butch Harmon was the first sign that changes were on the way for 1999.

Around this time, Se Ri got it into her head that, despite wins in two majors, Leadbetter had not done all he could in 1998 to advance her career. In November, prior to the LPGA Tour Championship in Las Vegas, Se Ri met with "swing doctor" Butch Harmon and played a round with his most famous pupil, Tiger Woods. A few weeks later, Leadbetter was dismissed.

Se Ri had also had enough of the South Korean media. She recognized that the relationship between reporters and athletes is different in South Korea than it is in the United States. In her country, the sporting press is more demanding, and expects athletes to make their lives easier. That arrangement worked fine until Se Ri came along. Because the South Korean media never had an athlete of her stature to cover, however, they did not understand how nerve-wracking their behavior could be. After Se Ri's LPGA Championship win, for instance, they hounded her, often calling for interviews in the middle of the night. When Se Ri entered the hospital in Seoul, TV cameramen barged right into her room without even asking for permission. They began filming her, half-dressed, with wires and tubes coming out of every part of her body. Enough was enough, she decided. Things would have to change.

In 1999, Se Ri really started putting her foot down—softly at first, so as not to show a lack of respect for her father and business partners—but she was definitely starting to assume control of her life. She hired the powerful International Management Group to represent her, which limited her father's power, put a buffer between herself and Samsung, and gave her a way to filter the hundreds of requests that come her way each week. Se Ri also reworked the details of her deal with Samsung, so that she would earn more, get hassled less, and also be free to negotiate separate endorsement deals for shoes and equipment.

Se Ri took another symbolic step toward independence when she bought a house in Orlando. She is mostly there alone or with her older sister, Yoo Ri, and she likes it that way. Se Ri lives in a neighborhood where she can walk and shop and eat without everyone rushing up to her for her autograph. And that suits her just fine, too. "In Korea, when I go somewhere, many people want to talk to me," she says. "This is more comfortable for me. I can practice more and focus on golf. I don't feel like a visitor anymore. This is a wonderful country. I'm here to stay."

What lies ahead for Se Ri? She is capable of accomplishing almost anything. Her swing is magnificent, which is a tribute both to David Leadbetter and Se Ri's own remarkable natural ability. In fact, from the tee to the green, her game is almost unimprovable. Her putting could use a little more consistency, but that generally comes with experience.

The really hard work for Se Ri will not take place on the golf course, but in her own mind. She is just now learning that she is an independent young woman whose gifts extend beyond the 18th hole—and that her thoughts and feelings really do matter. Those who know her are convinced she will find a way to honor her father, serve her game, and blend two very different cultures together in a way that works best for her. It may take a

"I am not number one yet, but I have a good start."
SE RI PAK

One of Se Ri's big hopes for the future is that the South Korean media will give her some breathing room as her career develops. Their constant demands are a major reason she has decided to live in the United States during the LPGA Tour's off-season.

while—and she may go through some rough times while she finds her way—but that is part of growing up, whether you are a young golf star or just a young person.

Fortunately, Se Ri now has the right people in her corner. She is beginning to make friends, and is getting advice from people who have been down the same road—people like Nancy Lopez, who has become less of a mommy and more of a mentor. Se Ri will learn that she really can set the ground rules for the media. She will learn that she really *can* sit and sign autographs for a few minutes instead of a few hours. She *can* determine her own practice schedule, and pick the events she will play. And she *can* live her own life.

For Se Ri's fans, the fun will be seeing how long her LPGA résumé will grow. For Se Ri's friends, it will be fun to watch her grow. "This is a good start," Se Ri says of her early success, "but I'm not finished yet. I want to be the best. That is my dream."

Will Se Ri follow in the footsteps of her hero, Nancy Lopez?
For now, she is happy to have Nancy at her side, as a friend and adviser.

Index